BY THE SAME AUTHOR

Fiction
And I Shall Be Healed

Plays (Published by Lazy Bee Scripts)
Limbo
Pilate's Wife
Mirror Image

Dramatic Monologues
Untold Lives: a collection of monologues for performance

~

Ladies' Night

~

Julia Lee Dean

Quickbeam Press

First published by Quickbeam Press

A catalogue record for this book is available from the British Library.

Edited by Mike Rose-Steel
Typeset in Garamond by Tricia Kristufek

Cover design by www.jdsmith-design.com

Print Edition
ISBN-13: 978-0-9927709-3-8

Caution

DEDICATION

To Virginia Byron and Stephanie Felton for taking a
chance and coming to Belfast with *Reflections*. A thoroughly
enjoyable production.

.

CONTENTS

ACKNOWLEDGMENTS

Thanks to:

My editor, Mike Rose-Steel, for his unceasing attention to detail.

My typesetter, Tricia Kristufek, for her patience with my amendments.

Virginia Byron, Caryl Jones, and Karim Kronfli for creating the roles of Margot, Natasha, and Mirror and, in Karim's case, for directing the premiere of *Mirror, Mirror,* also to Stephanie Felton for directing the premiere of *Reflections (When Maggie Met Margot).*

Thanks also to all my actress friends for complaining about the lack of roles for women. I hope you find something in this collection that you can use.

REFLECTIONS

REFLECTIONS

(when Maggie met Margot)

First performed by Wired to the Moon Productions at the Spectrum Centre, Shankill Road, Belfast, on 22nd October 2011 as part of the Belfast Fringe Festival, with the following cast:

Margot...................................... Julia Lee Dean
Maggie......................................Virginia Byron

Directed by Stephanie Felton

Technical crew provided by the Spectrum Centre.

CHARACTERS OF THE PLAY

Margot: female, 20s – 30s. A stand-up comic. NB the year of birth referred to in the play should be adjusted to approximate that of the actress cast.

Maggie: female, 40 +. Margot's older self

The standup set performed by Margot's character on pages 4-6 was written and performed by the author at stand up venues at London and Edinburgh in 2010 and can be viewed on YouTube.

[*Dressing room. Table and two chairs, one on either side. A makeup mirror stands on the table amid a mess of tissues, magazines and makeup. Maggie, enters SL, wearing a cowled cloak. Maggie walks into room. Stands and looks about her.*]

MAGGIE: What a place to come back to. Of all the beautiful places in my life, this is the one I choose to revisit. My own choice! A theatre dressing room at a comedy festival; when I think how thrilled I was to get this place, my own dressing room! I wasn't one of the chorus girls any more, I was the star! In fact [*Exits briefly, comes back holding a home-made paper star and stands looking at it*] I'd seen far too many films. It's just embarrassing to think of now. Silly cow, I thought I'd made it, I was sure I'd be rich and famous: it was all there waiting for me if only I could free myself from the everyday my dreams would come true! I didn't have a clue. I already had everything I could ever want, everything I would ever want and there I was, chasing the one thing that didn't matter. [*Pause*] I want to blame someone: if only someone had warned me but, if I'm honest, Daniel tried and I didn't listen, too frightened of missing my shot at the big time. [*Pause*] Daniel [*Beat*] what I did to you is unforgiveable. I don't deserve this chance. But you do, my love, you do.

Where is she then? This Margot? Out on stage no doubt, basking in the laughter of strangers. No, I mustn't be too hard on her, though she ruined my life. Did they laugh that night? I can't remember. When I think back I always hear people laughing, but it's a cynical, gloating sort of laughter. Nothing to do with humour. Stop it, Maggie. I should forgive her, she's young. Fuck it, how many times have I heard that excuse? My life's in ruins because I was young once! There's never a swift kick up the arse when you need one, is there? Too many people are too quick to make allowances: *ah, leave her alone, she's young, she doesn't know any better, she'll learn.* Too bloody right she'll learn, but at what cost? It's even worse if she is in possession of a decent pair of tits; a buoyancy aid for life. *Ah, she has the looks, she'll be fine, no bother.* I sound bitter, I know I do. I don't mean to be, don't want to be but seeing this place again, remembering...what did any of it really matter? [*Rifles through make up & things on dressing table, picks up a card attached to some flowers & reads*] Knock 'em dead, I love you. Daniel kiss kiss kiss [*Holds card to her chest*] Daniel! Even to see your handwriting again! I will do what I can to make it right, my love, I promise. [*Sits down at the dressing table SL and looks about her*] Where is she? How much longer?

[*Black out. Maggie leans her head on the table, blending in with clothes heaped up. Lights up on Margot, on stage in behind a microphone.*]

MARGOT: Does anyone here remember those "Just say no" campaigns? We had something called PSVE at school: Personal, Social and Vocational Education. It was all condoms on carrots and how to say "no". And we were taught to say no to *everything*. Sex, drugs, cigarettes, … and I always felt that the teachers had missed the point. Such care taken to defend us from temptation; didn't they realise how *cool* you had to be at fourteen to be *offered* a cigarette? Imagine our disappointment when we finally left school only to find that the streets were not thronged with unwashed hordes dying to give you one (whatever that one might be)? And it doesn't get better as you get older, it gets worse. Nowadays I don't even have to say "no" to get rid of a guy. I simply tell him my age. Because when I say 32 – 32 – 32 what men hear is "tick – tick – tick". Because obviously, now that I'm in my thirties I must be desperate to settle down and have children [*Pause*]. This was news to me and right now the prospect is not an attractive one. I've got it pretty good and yes, I may be husband hunting [*Beat*] but that doesn't mean I want one of my own. Still, it would be nice to have someone to fetch the spiders out of the bath for me so, after much wailing and gnashing of teeth, I went to a Singles Night.

Has anyone here ever been to a Singles Night? Horrible aren't they? And I think the reason I find them so awful is because I've misunderstood what they're for. A Singles Night, ladies and gentlemen, is not designed to save us from the single state. Oh no, it is to remind us that we're better off there.

Because there are two types of guy at a Singles Night. First the adorers. These guys fall in love at first sight and prostrate themselves in front of you, begging you not to hurt them. Frankly I find that quite irritating, because it impedes my progress to the bar. Now, I'm not one for walking over men but when there's a gin and tonic in the offing I can't guarantee I'll always go round. Then there are the James Bonds. These guys are so totally in denial that they're at a Singles Night that they will try and make you feel grateful for their attention while they lean in, all teeth and Rolexes and you smile, lean away and wonder why there's never an ejector seat when you want one.

Because let's face it. Romance is dead, isn't it? And it's disappointing if you've grown up watching those films from the 1950s where a guy actually asked a girl out. He'd turn up at her house in his car with an oversized box of chocolates. All in Glorious Technicolor. Now the first hint you get that a guy likes you is finding his tongue halfway down your esophagus and there you are, bent backwards on the baize of a pub pool table thinking, "What? No chocolates?"

[*Beat*] Thank you, I've been Margot and you've been terrific. I want you to go home now and tell your loved ones the three most important words in life. That's right, ladies, Mid Season Sale. Good night!

[*Margot sets the mic to one side SR and sits down in the chair SR where she examines her face in the mirror. She picks up her phone from the table and peers at the screen then puts it to her ear.*]

MARGOT: Hello? Were you trying to ring? I had it on silent, I was on stage. Yeah it was good, they weren't bad tonight. I thought you were coming to watch. Oh, you promised… Where? Oh I don't know, I don't want to eat too much…oh, alright then, will you meet me downstairs? I won't be long, I just have to do my face. OK, bye!

[*She puts down the phone and starts to contort her face into a series of face-tightening exercises with her eyes closed. Maggie sits up and faces Margot. Margot turns back towards the mirror and finds herself staring into Maggie's face.*]

MARGOT: Aargh! [*grasps face*]

MAGGIE: Sorry, did I make you jump?

MARGOT: Oh, you're real. Thank God. I thought my moisturiser had let me down. [*Continues to pat and fidget with her face*]

MAGGIE: I was hoping to have a word with you.

MARGOT: Just one? I do hope it's "television".

MAGGIE: Pardon?

MARGOT: Well, if that Sarah Millican can get Live at the Apollo *and* Radio 4, I don't see why I shouldn't have a bash. After all, I'm much better looking that she is, don't you think?

MAGGIE: Not really, no.

MARGOT: Oh. Well, I suppose eyesight starts to dim at your age but I can assure you it's true. And, let's face it, appearances are everything. The art of celebrity.

MAGGIE: Not really an art though, is it? It's all a work of fiction. Harmless enough as long as you're not daft enough to believe in it.

MARGOT: Oh I know, of course you're quite right really, but look at this [B*randishes magazine*].

MAGGIE: Oh no, not this rubbish. You do know that these things are full of nothing but wannabes and nobodies.

Margot: Not true! [*Beat*] I'm in it.

MAGGIE: Oh God, I'd forgotten about that.

MARGOT: Listen, it says [*Reading*] "Up and coming comic, Margot" – that's me – "Looked pale and tired leaving her boyfriend's flat on Monday morning…"

MAGGIE: I remember those Sunday nights.

MARGOT: "It is rumoured that the couple may be heading for a split. Margot has cited career pressure…" Isn't that dramatic?

MAGGIE: But it's not true. [*Beat*] It doesn't have to be true.

MARGOT: Well, no, although it did get me thinking.

MAGGIE: Oh no, please…

MARGOT: We *have* been together a long time now. Perhaps it's getting a bit too comfortable.

MAGGIE: No.

MARGOT: A year is practically a lifetime these days and the thing with comedy is that you need to hook up with the Zeitgeist or whatever. Just look around you, all these stunning women still single because they can't find a man who wants a woman and not an X-box. Nobody chats anyone up any more; a man won't even buy a girl a drink nowadays for fear there's a wedding ring at the bottom of the glass. I'm missing all that: I've got the most gorgeous, perfect boyfriend who loves me. I can't relate to my target audience and that has an impact on my career. I'd be a fool to keep him.

MAGGIE: [*Aside*] I actually remember coming out with all this crap. Hard to believe I believed it. [*To Margot*] No one will ever love you more.

MARGOT: How do you know that?

MAGGIE: I just know

MARGOT: Do you tell fortunes?

MAGGIE: Some fortunes.

MARGOT: Oh goody [*Extends hand*].

MAGGIE: [*Ignoring hand*] You will have children [*Beat*] But I think you already know that.

MARGOT: [*Snatching back her hand*] No.

MAGGIE: No?

MARGOT: They destroy your figure and eat your money. Anyway, it's not the right time.

MAGGIE: It's later than you think.

MARGOT: Rubbish! 30 is the new 15! That makes it practically illegal. My time is now. This won't last you know.

MAGGIE: Oh I know, believe me, I know. And what'll be waiting for you when this is all over? When you're just a former comic, an almost-was, sitting at home watching someone else on the telly - who'll be there to laugh along beside you?

MARGOT: Do you know how long it's taken me to get here? I didn't have the self-belief at twenty I…I'd had a hard time, you know?

MAGGIE: So you were bullied at school! Who wasn't? It was the eighties, ritual humiliation was part of the curriculum. It's about time you got over it.

MARGOT: Nobody can spit on you when you're standing up on stage. For the first time in my life I'm going home with dry hair.

MAGGIE: Tell it to the tabloids, darling, no one else is interested.

MARGOT: So you think the tabloids would be? [*Beat*] I could write my autobiography! Everyone does that nowadays. I could serialise it in the Mail - write it in "real-time."

MAGGIE: That's a diary.

MARGOT: Only old men write diaries. I'm young! I should be writing my autobiography. Is that why you're here?

MAGGIE: I won a competition.

MARGOT: To meet me? Cor [*Beat*] shouldn't I have been told about that? [*Brandishes magazine*] *They* should have been told about that. There should be photographers, PR people, fees…

MAGGIE: Not to meet you. Not exactly. It was an essay competition entitled "What I would say to my younger self". I entered and won.

[*Silence*]

MAGGIE: So here I am.

MARGOT: I'm the prize?

MAGGIE: If that's the way you'd like to see it then, yes. The way the competition works is that the entrants write down what they would say to their younger selves. The prize is that the winner gets to say it.

MARGOT: So, where do I come in?

MAGGIE: You're my younger self [*Produces script and prepares to read*] "Dear Margot, I don't mind calling you that although we both know your name is Maggie…"

MARGOT: What?

MAGGIE: Ssh, I worked hard on this, it's deeply heartfelt and I really want you to follow my advice.

MARGOT: I don't understand. Who are you? [*Beat*] What was that bit about your younger self?

MAGGIE: My name is Margaret Cooke.

MARGOT: But that's…

MAGGIE: Go on, admit it.

MARGOT: That's my name too. But I prefer Margot. That's quite a coincidence.

MAGGIE: No. No coincidence, we're the same person, you and I.

MARGOT: I don't think so. I mean, look at you.

MAGGIE: Years of addiction.

MARGOT: Really? Drink or drugs?

MAGGIE: Botox. It was the cause of all my problems. Still, a stiff upper lip and all that...

MARGOT: I don't believe that.

MAGGIE: No, I mean it. It's very hard to be taken seriously when you look surprised all the time. And my sex life just disappeared, men can be so sensitive.

MARGOT: [*Looking* around] There's a hidden camera around here somewhere, isn't there?

MAGGIE: No.

MARGOT: Oh really? So you're what I'm going to look like in twenty years' time? This has to be a joke.

MAGGIE: Ten.

MARGOT: Make that a nightmare. I don't believe you. I can't [*Snatches up the mirror*] My life will be over.

MAGGIE: Believe me or not, it won't change anything. In ten years' time you will be sitting where I am now, looking at – you. Unless you listen to me now. [*Beat*] On the plus side, you become a lot more tactful. [*Beat*] What have you got there?

11

MARGOT: My own self.

MAGGIE: You are more than skin deep.

MARGOT: Oh no I'm not. What you see is what you get. My face is my fortune.

MAGGIE: [*Looking*] What's that? That's not even your face! [*Tears picture from mirror*]

MARGOT: Yes it is!

MAGGIE: It's a photograph [*Beat*] That's not me…us.

MARGOT: Yes.

MAGGIE: It's been airbrushed!

MARGOT: It's still me.

MAGGIE: No. It's an image of how you would look if everything human was stripped away. Look at it, you're like something out of Star Trek!

MARGOT: [*Snatching back photo*] Is that what you've always wanted to say to your younger self? That she looks like something out of Star Trek?

MAGGIE: Not exactly.

MARGOT: Very profound I must say, travelling through time and space just to heap abuse on your younger self.

MAGGIE: I'd forgotten I was such a silly cow.

MARGOT: Silly? Me? My older self suddenly appears in my dressing room masquerading as a Scottish widow – don't think I didn't notice the cloak – and how do I react? Do I freak out, run screaming down the

corridor or lunge at you with my hair straighteners?
No I do not [*Pause*] though you must admit this is a bit
weird.

MAGGIE: I know, I can't believe it either. [*Beat*] I never
win anything.

MARGOT: Can I have my photo back?

MAGGIE: It's not your photo.

MARGOT: Yes it is.

MAGGIE: What is the point of looking in the mirror at a
photograph?

MARGOT: I like the way I look in it.

MAGGIE: It isn't you.

MARGOT: It's me *plus*. The improved version; digitally
remastered.

MAGGIE: Digitally masked more like. Where did it come
from?

MARGOT: I cut it out of a magazine. An article on up-and-
coming comics.

MAGGIE: [*Picking up magazine*] Like this one?

MARGOT: It was a good article.

MAGGIE: [*Flipping through magazine*] You do realise that
none of these people are real?

MARGOT: Don't be silly [*pointing*] I saw her in Camden last
week.

MAGGIE: Did she look like that?

MARGOT: Well, no, but it was a Saturday morning.

MAGGIE: So?

MARGOT: A Saturday morning means there's been a Friday night [*Beat*] no one looks good after a Friday night.

MAGGIE: Unless they've been airbrushed. Everyone in here looks like they've stepped straight out of Rivendell. It's like Tolkien porn!

MARGOT: You're some sort of crazed fan.

MAGGIE: Doesn't it bother you that the image your allegedly adoring public have of you doesn't look anything like you? You want to be remembered but no one knows what you really look like. It's like you've gone undercover in your own life. No one in this magazine really exists; they are figments of a flabby imagination. Why should anyone pay good money to read this crap? Made up stories about made up people whose, non-existent look you can "get" if you consult the style oracle on page 45.

MARGOT: There's nothing wrong with having heroes.

MARGOT: No, but they should be admired for what they are, not for what they are not. You're thrilled that they've stuck you in these pages but do you even know who you are?

MARGOT: Of course I do. Don't be ridiculous.

MAGGIE: Alright then, tell me five things about yourself.

MARGOT: My name is Margot Canard.

MAGGIE: Margaret Cooke.

MARGOT: What's in a name? A rose by any other name…

MAGGIE: You're not a rose. Come on, more.

MARGOT: I'm twenty-seven years old.

MAGGIE: What year were you born?

MARGOT: Nineteen seventy… oh now that's not fair!

MAGGIE: Ha! I knew I'd get on you on the maths. What else?

MARGOT: Erm… [*Pause, Margot thinks then sees magazine open at "her" page and makes a grab for it – reading*] I'm a keen sportswoman, enjoy fine wines and long walks with my dog.

MAGGIE: You haven't got a dog, your idea of a fine wine is one someone else has paid for and hunting for the TV remote is not a sport. [*Beat*] I came here to talk to my younger self, to impart deeply resonant words of advice, and I find that she doesn't exist.

MARGOT: [*Looking down at herself*] Yes I do.

MAGGIE: No, it's not you sitting there. It's some celebrity construct; the scraped together remnants of 1980s materialism and Tony Blair's Cool Britannia.

MARGOT: Celebrity?

MAGGIE: [*Ignoring her*] Just another cardboard cut-out for whom a push up bra is a career move. [*Margot looks down at & adjusts her cleavage*] How could I have been so stupid? What was the point of all this? [*Brandishes her essay*] All this work and you won't even listen. I just don't remember being such an airhead. I suppose I wouldn't; we all go through life believing that we're the good guys. How else could we go on? [*Looks at Margot*] But how did this silly bitch get to have such power over my life? Oh Daniel! If only we'd met later when I could understand what I'd found in you. I had hoped that I could change things by coming here. I'm so sorry, my love.

MARGOT: It's the first sign of madness, you know.

MAGGIE: What is?

MARGOT: Talking to yourself.

[*Silence, they look at each other.*]

MAGGIE: If you leave Daniel you'll regret it.

MARGOT: I'm too young to settle down and disappear! I've worked too hard. I gave up my weekends to homework and for what?

MAGGIE: All those Latin Sundays

MARGOT:}

MAGGIE} Without the cha-cha-cha!

[*They render this line in different ways and look at each other in surprise. Maggie sees her chance.*]

MAGGIE: But none that will love you as he loves you. You may think you want to be free and single again but you love him more than you know, you need him too. Turn your back on him and you will regret it for the rest of your life. It will be a wound that never heals and it will throb every time you remember that the sense of loss you wake up to every morning is your own doing. No amount of sex and alcohol will dull that pain. I can promise you that.

MARGOT: [*Pause*] You should write for Mills and Boon.

MAGGIE: Listen to me!

MARGOT: I suppose it's difficult not to get sentimental at your age. I prefer the philosophical approach. [*Sententiously*] It is better to have loved and lost than never to have loved at all.

MAGGIE: Bollocks. It is better to have love and lust, every night if possible, and twice on Sunday.

MARGOT: Well, there is that I suppose.

MAGGIE: You are your own worst enemy. You're all set to ditch your boyfriend to feel more at one with your audience and all the time you're allowing your photographs to be airbrushed so that you look like another species altogether. You don't know what you want.

MARGOT: I don't want to get sucked into his life and lose myself in him. I want to be me. I've worked hard to make it this far, I don't want to lose that and end up just someone's wife [*Beat*] and someone else's mother.

MAGGIE: Better than being no one's wife.

MARGOT: How very Victorian! Didn't you hear about the sexual revolution?

MAGGIE: Did you? Look at what you're wearing.

MARGOT: Oh, this is just a costume. You know, my professional philosophy: the jokes are for the girls so… [*Maggie joins in*] the men might as well have something to look at.

MAGGIE: [*Aside*] Good grief [*to Margot*] Something?

You've given them everything!

MARGOT: No, just a little hint, something for their imagination to work on.

MAGGIE: Believe me, they don't have to work that hard. Tell me, are the false eyelashes really necessary? You look like something out of a Carry-On.

MARGOT: Oh, I'd die without my falsies.

MAGGIE: Why? Do they bring you food? You die without food, drink, warmth and love. Everything else is just decoration.

MARGOT: You don't *die* without love!

MAGGIE: Oh I think you do. Some part of you does. I think everybody has a certain amount of love in them, some more, some less. The ability to love is what makes us human. There's joy in being loved but loving another person is what keeps us going. Yet if there's no outlet for it, if we have no one to love, it grows stale and becomes a burden to that person. It chafes against their very soul and life loses its radiance.

MARGOT: Blimey. Maybe you should get a cat. [*Phone rings*] Hi Daniel, where are you?… I won't be long… yes I know but I've got someone with me…[*Sighs*]…well go in and order if you're hungry. Oh alright but I might be a while yet…ok, bye.

MAGGIE: You'll kill him, you know.

MARGOT: Who?

MAGGIE: Daniel.

MARGOT: Oh God, how? [*Beat*] Does it get into the

papers? Is that why you're here? You're some sort of psychic.

MAGGIE: He won't die, not literally, but he will cease to live, in a way. You will know your mistake as soon as you've made it but it will be too late; there'll be no going back.

MARGOT: No, don't be silly. Daniel knows me well enough. I'm the creative type, he likes that.

MAGGIE: You'll go too far this time. A person can only take so much. He's sitting downstairs right now, waiting for you. He's dressed up, nervous and it will be the last time you ever see him.

MARGOT: Where's he going?

MAGGIE: Precisely nowhere. Not now.

MARGOT: Am I going somewhere? Is this my big break?

MAGGIE: I suppose so, in a manner of speaking.

MARGOT: You don't mean he's going to dump me? Oh the shame! [*Aside*] but I could gag it, couldn't I? Make it funny?

MAGGIE: I couldn't. I still can't. I was cruel to him, so panicked by the thought of my lost freedom. I always thought I was too good for him but in the end I didn't deserve him.

MARGOT: Oh give over, it's been ten years for you. It sounds like you're still not over it.

[*Maggie doesn't reply, avoids Margot's gaze. When Margot tries to look into her face She turns away then gets up and crosses SL, away from the table.*]

MARGOT: Something I said? [*Beat*] Are you alright?

[*Maggie turns and comes back to seat, the heels of her hands held to her eyes. She turns stage front, takes deep breath and sits down.*]

MARGOT: Are you alright?

MAGGIE: Yes, yes I'm fine. [*Sighs*] Sometimes I really wished I smoked, you know?

MARGOT: I've got pear drops somewhere.

MAGGIE: [*Shakes her head*] It doesn't matter. It's just, well, some things you don't get over. Some things you don't forget, can't forget. Guilt is its own penance.

MARGOT: Is this still about Daniel?

MAGGIE: [*Aside*] Not just Daniel [*To Margot*] I'm sorry if I'm boring you.

MARGOT: No, really, I want to know. What do I do to him?

MAGGIE: You… No, I shouldn't do this. Look I'll just read you my essay and go, eh? He's waiting for you, poor man, [*aside*] if only he knew.

MARGOT: Knew what?

[*Silence*]

MAGGIE: That you are unfaithful.

MARGOT: Am I? [*Beat*] Who with?

MAGGIE: With this [*Gestures with her hand at the stage, audience*]. You' sell your soul for a round of applause.

MARGOT: I would not! [*Beat*] A standing ovation, at least.

MAGGIE: Some people live their whole lives without ever stepping on a stage. A fair number of them never even think of it.

MARGOT: Some people end up in prison.

MAGGIE: The two are not related.

MARGOT: Is there a point to this?

MAGGIE: It just occurred to me. Do you really think you're good?

MARGOT: Me? Ah well… [*Mumbles*]

MAGGIE: What?

MARGOT: Does it matter? It's not really about being *good* is it?

MAGGIE: Isn't it?

MARGOT: It's about exposure, getting some, I mean; if you look good on camera and wear the right clothes, know the right people, it'll just happen. If people know your name they'll just assume you're good at something even if they don't know what that is.

MAGGIE: You don't like doing this do you? You just want to be famous.

MARGOT: It's a means to an end.

MAGGIE: What end?

MARGOT: I want to be somebody.

MAGGIE: You are somebody. You're Margaret Cooke.

MARGOT: But I want them to *know* I'm somebody. I want

them to see me on telly and wonder what they did with their lives.

MAGGIE: Who's them?

MARGOT: I want to be invited back to my old school to give uplifting talks about female achievement and to be able to say "No, I won't come back. You never helped me so I'm not going to help you now!"

MAGGIE: You're still in the playground, aren't you?

MARGOT: Every time I drive past that school I look at that building and think, "Just you wait, you bastards, I'll show you."

MAGGIE: They're not there anymore. It's an empty building.

MARGOT: I still remember.

MAGGIE: But those girls don't. They left, got jobs, got married. They've their own families. I doubt they'd recognise you now, even if you did roll up in a limousine with Johnny Depp on one arm and George Clooney on the other.

MARGOT: How did you…oh. You remember, of course you do. [*Maggie nods*] So you'll remember how it was: the whispers, the threats just because of where you lived? The way they would pretend they liked you just to get you to talk, the constant strain of having to be forever on your guard. Watching what you said and who you said it to. At ten years old.

MAGGIE: That's twenty-odd years ago.

MARGOT: Yes well, suspicion becomes a habit. When a person comes over all friendly there's usually an ulterior motive there somewhere. You must know that yourself.

MAGGIE: No, in fact as I go through life I am constantly surprised at how wrong I was about that.

MARGOT: Hmpfh.

MAGGIE: You want revenge and you're giving up your life to take it. A classic case of Revenger's tragedy. Those girls have already won, you do realise that? They're not ten years old anymore. They've gone and got on with things. It's you that can't move on. It's pathetic. It's about time you stopped being so self-obsessed or you're going to end up very lonely indeed.

MARGOT: I have moved on, I just want to be better than them. It's me alone against the world. Always was, always will be. I don't need them, I don't need anyone. [*Beat*] I just want to be better than I am.

MAGGIE: There's nothing wrong with you now. The grass isn't always greener.

MARGOT: Tell me about Daniel.

MAGGIE: Why don't you like doing this?

MARGOT: [*Shrugs*] It's just me up there, trying to entertain people who are too cool to be seen laughing in public. The gigs are late and…

MAGGIE: Daniel always comes though?

MARGOT: He didn't tonight.

MAGGIE: Ah well, he'll tell you about that.

MARGOT: Tell me about him.

MAGGIE: I can't. I'm not allowed, it was in the competition smallprint.

MARGOT: Oh, space time continuum and all that?

MAGGIE: Dunno, they just said that was cheating – not in the spirit of the thing, apparently. I can't tell you the lottery numbers either.

MARGOT: Oh.

MAGGIE: Not that I can remember them, I didn't gen up on lucrative titbits before I came through that door.

MARGOT: Shame. [*Beat*] So, you can't tell me anything?

MAGGIE: Have you ever read in a book the phrase "I watched as a variety of emotions passed across his face"?

MARGOT: Back to the Mills and Boon again.

MAGGIE: I never realised it was actually possible to see emotions fight like that but the last time I saw Daniel I saw disbelief, shock and such disappointment! It was as though he'd been told he had to lose a limb. In my vanity I thought I'd delivered a nice little speech: a gentle let down, all soft voice and soulful eyes, but when I saw his face I suddenly realised that I was out of my depth. Yet he was the one drowning. He seemed to fade away before my eyes, the romantic gloom of the place seemed to suck all the colour out of his face. Afterwards he still insisted on paying for dinner, though he couldn't look at me.

MARGOT: But you were free. All the times before, I was relieved to finish with a guy, it was like I was getting my life back.

MAGGIE: This time it was different. I didn't feel free, I felt lost. I had cut myself adrift and no amount of regret would reverse the current; with him I hadn't been tied down, just secured.

MARGOT: But Daniel's Daniel, we'll still be friends and who knows, perhaps in time... [*Sees Maggie shaking her head*] No?

MAGGIE: No. I think he tried but he couldn't do it.

MARGOT: Couldn't or wouldn't?

MAGGIE: Either way I can't blame him. All our Facebook updates? Trying to prove we hadn't made a mistake, it's not surprising he blocked us in the end.

MARGOT: Well, that just goes to show, he wasn't for me...us.

MAGGIE: He was hurt! He wanted you to come after him, not be confronted with evidence that you were moving on. The sad thing is you weren't moving on, not really. [*Pause*] He found out about the other thing. If you still decide to go ahead, tell him or tell no one.

[*Phone rings*]

MARGOT: [*Picking up phone*] I'm coming Daniel! Yes, don't you want me to look nice? Oh? Oh, alright then. I'll be down shortly. [*Puts phone down*] Oh how he nags! I just wish he'd leave me alone.

MAGGIE: You will live to regret those words.

MARGOT: Will I? Why don't you just tell me what you're trying to tell me? It's like fortune-telling by numbers, this. It's getting on my nerves and, in case you haven't noticed, the man himself is waiting downstairs for me.

It's too much. I can't think straight any more. I just want it to stop!

MAGGIE: Why don't I go down and ask him to wait?

MARGOT: What?

MAGGIE: I just want to see him. He won't recognise me. I could always tell him I'm an aunt or something but, oh to see his face again; to see him young and well, what I wouldn't give to have that chance, just for a moment. I miss him so much.

MARGOT: You don't still see him? I can't imagine not seeing him, I couldn't never see him again.

MAGGIE: Not even once after this night. Why else do you think I am here? This is the crucial moment in your life and I'm hoping I can change our future for the better.

MARGOT: Oh, that bad is it?

MAGGIE: No, it's not bad. Quite successful even, but it could be happier. At least, I hope it could be happier. It could definitely be different.

MARGOT: All because of what I do tonight?

MAGGIE: I reckon so.

MARGOT: This competition, did you have to choose the point you'd want to come back to?

MAGGIE: Yes, I had to choose my moment and then explain why I felt this was the turning point in my life and what I wish I'd done differently, then it was just a matter of writing down what I wanted to say to you…me.

MARGOT: Have you said it all?

MAGGIE: [*Picks up her essay and flicks through it*] Well, not in order, obviously. When I wrote it I hadn't really bargained on being constantly interrupted.

MARGOT: Ah, you know me.

MAGGIE: [*Still flicking*] Let's see, I've said that…that…that…I've more or less said that…I don't think I'll bother saying that [*Glancing at Margot*]…yes…yes…and yes…[*Pause*].

MARGOT: [*Standing up*] All done?

MAGGIE: There's one more thing.

MARGOT: Go on then, but make it quick, I've got to go.

MAGGIE: You will miss the friend longer than you'll miss the lover.

MARGOT: [*Nodding*] Is that everything?

MAGGIE: I think so. [*Watches Margot putting on her coat*] Margot?

MARGOT: Yes?

MAGGIE: The decision you're trying to make is not for you alone. You're frightened of how he'll react: maybe he'll run, maybe he won't. Right now you don't even know which possibility frightens you more but don't push him away. At least talk to him.

MARGOT: This isn't how I imagined things. I always thought I'd know what to do, that everything would happen at my pace in the correct order. I hate not being in control. I feel so angry!

MAGGIE: But you are in control! Be angry if you must but don't cut off your nose to spite your face. There's no shame in letting things happen. You're still the person you are; you will never be anyone else, so you need to make sure you're someone you can live with. You don't have to give up your career, if that's really what this is, but don't give up everything else. If its photographs you're after, isn't it better to be photographed holding your baby than stumbling out of some nightclub with your knickers around your ankles? For the first time in your life you're not on your own. That man downstairs is waiting for you because it's you he wants. No ulterior motive, no cruel joke, apart from the one you're about to play on him. You're luckier than most, so have the good sense you were born with and know when you're well off. Not everybody gets this chance.

[*Pause. They look at each other. Margot is about to say something when the phone in her hand rings. She smiles at Maggie and answers it.*]

MARGOT: Hi Daniel… yes I'm sorry, I'm coming now…look, darling, would you mind if we didn't go out? I'm really tired and, well, how about we just get a take away and snuggle up on the sofa. I could do with a chat…yeah…well, maybe not the wine. [*She puts the phone in her pocket and smiles at Maggie.*] So I suppose this is it then?

MAGGIE: Reckon so.

MARGOT: What happens now?

MAGGIE: You get on with your life and I go through that door and back to mine.

MARGOT: I hope it's better for you.

MAGGIE: I think it might be.

MARGOT: Well, goodbye…Maggie.

MAGGIE: Goodbye. [*Margot turns towards exit SR.*] By the way…

MARGOT: [*turning*] Yes?

MAGGIE: If Daniel asks you something tonight, say yes.

[*Margot smiles, waves and exits. Maggie stands looking after her then turns centre stage standing alert as if listening for something. After a moment she smiles.*]

MAGGIE: Yes. Better.

BLACKOUT

MIRROR, MIRROR

MIRROR, MIRROR

First performed by The Goats Theatre Company Ltd at Ye Olde Rose and Crown Theatre Pub, Walthamstow, London, on 31ˢᵗ October 2011, with the following cast:

Natasha...Caryl Jones
Mirror...Karim Kronfli

Directed by Karim Kronfli

CHARACTERS OF THE PLAY

Natasha: female; 30 - 60
Mirror: male or female; any age. The actor is never seen, only the voice is heard.

[*Natasha sits, centre stage, at her dressing table in front of a large mirror. There is an (unseen) window downstage left, looking out towards the audience, and an (unseen) door downstage right. Natasha is dressed up and making-up her face, singing along to the stereo (perhaps Janis Joplin, perhaps "Another Little Piece of My Heart"). After a few moments she stops and really looks at herself in the mirror. The music fades. Slowly, she raises a hand to her face.*]

NATASHA: Sometimes there just isn't enough make-up in the world. [*Pause, with the hand that is at her face, she reaches out and touches her reflection in the glass*] That face... reminds me of someone... They say that mirrors can house the ghosts of the past... can that really be me? [*Beat*] Don't be silly Nat! You're just getting older, don't be morbid. It's about time you stopped being so vain, that's all. [*Sighs*] Mirror, Mirror on the wall, who is the fairest of them all?

MIRROR: Well it isn't you, darlin'. Not anymore, though to be honest, looks were never really your strong point.

NATASHA: I thought it was the light that was meant to be harsh.

MIRROR: Not at this time of day, so you don't need that much make-up, surely? [*Natasha doesn't respond*] You look like you've been given a make-over by a mortician. [*Pause*] Do you remember your grandmother?

NATASHA: I'm going out.

MIRROR: Ah that's nice. Husband treating you, is he?

NATASHA: He is, as a matter of fact. It's ages since we've been out together.

MIRROR: You sound nervous.

32

NATASHA: No. I'm excited. It's going to be a good night.

MIRROR: As long as he stays off the drink.

NATASHA: He will, he's promised.

MIRROR: And you believe him?

NATASHA: [*Pause*] I do, actually, yes.

MIRROR: Then you are a fool my dear.

NATASHA: I beg your pardon?

MIRROR: It's disappointing. You had such promise. I expected great things of you.

NATASHA: Oh, did you?

MIRROR: Do you remember your grandmother?

NATASHA: What time is it? Tony'll be here soon. He's booked us a table for 7 o'clock.

MIRROR: Somewhere nice?

NATASHA: Yes, it's a French place, called *L'Escargot*.

MIRROR: Funny how a common garden pest sounds expensive and desirable when you say it in French.

NATASHA: Yes, I suppose it is.

MIRROR: I wonder, would it work as well for cockroach?

NATASHA: I don't know.

MIRROR: No. Still, get the packaging right and it's surprising what people will swallow.

NATASHA: Appearances are everything.

MIRROR: Tell me about your grandmother.

NATASHA: She gave me this house.

MIRROR: What else?

NATASHA: Nothing else.

MIRROR: You don't remember?

NATASHA: No.

MIRROR: You do, but you're afraid.

NATASHA: What of?

MIRROR: You tell me.

NATASHA: My grandmother is dead. There is nothing to be gained now in bringing up the past.

MIRROR: I came into this house when your grandmother married. I was a gift from her husband. He got her house. Just think of that. What was hers became his.

NATASHA: So?

MIRROR: So three generations of women have puckered, tweezed and wept before me. None have changed as much as you.

NATASHA: The times we live in.

MIRROR: I don't mean your hair or your hemline, sweetheart, but *you*. Not to put too fine a point on it, darlin', but where are you?

NATASHA: I'm right here.

MIRROR: Are you? You seem to have disappeared of late.

NATASHA: I'm right here in front of you. I can see my reflection in your glass.

MIRROR: But that's all it is, a reflection. How do you know it's really you? Can you still see yourself? Where's the woman of flesh and blood? She has faded away over the years. I see nothing left but a shade.

NATASHA: A shade?

Mirror: An echo of a life never lived, a purgatorial soul. What happened to all that ambition? All those things you wanted to be?

NATASHA: What things?

MIRROR: I remember you telling your grandmother. You were going to be a lawyer, a vet or a waitress.

NATASHA: A waitress?

MIRROR: Yes, well, I thought that one was a bit odd but you were only eleven.

NATASHA: I was a silly girl.

MIRROR: You were a happy girl. You were going to live in a big house with lots of animals.

NATASHA: Well this is a big house.

MIRROR: And the animals?

NATASHA: Tony's allergic.

MIRROR: Ah, shame.

NATASHA: Yes. I'd have liked a nice little dog.

MIRROR: You should please yourself. It's not as if he's

ever home.

NATASHA: Oh no, I couldn't. He'd be so upset. It's the fur, you see, it sets him off.

MIRROR: You're very accommodating.

NATASHA: Marriage is all about give and take.

MIRROR: What does he give you?

NATASHA: I would be lost without him.

MIRROR: Would you? Would you really?

NATASHA: He's very thoughtful sometimes. When we were younger I used to attend all his business parties and office functions. He used to say I was his lucky charm but I grew to dread them. I was so shy! He understood without me having to explain. [*Beat*] He doesn't ask me to go any more.

MIRROR: You weren't always shy.

NATASHA: Oh I was. Mummy said I was just like grandma.

MIRROR: Ah yes. [*Beat*] Now do you remember?

NATASHA: I don't know, my memories of her are vague.

MIRROR: Yes?

NATASHA: She never raised her voice when she spoke. Sometimes it was difficult to hear her. She even moved around the house as though she was afraid of being caught.

MIRROR: Caught?

NATASHA: Caught out, or sight of, I don't know, just that… It was unnerving. She haunted the rooms like a ghost afraid of disturbing the dust… As I got older I began to be frightened by her [*Beat*] her eyes…

MIRROR: He's late.

NATASHA: What? [*Checking her watch*] Not very, perhaps he's been held up at work. I hope he doesn't get too worked up.

MIRROR: Indeed. He does have a temper, doesn't he?

NATASHA: It's not his fault; he has a very stressful job.

MIRROR: He still shouldn't do it.

NATASHA: He knows that. He doesn't mean to.

MIRROR: Do you ever think about what he has cost you?

NATASHA: What do you mean, cost me?

MIRROR: Your daughter.

NATASHA: Emma. [*Pause*] She was nineteen last week.

MIRROR: How long is it since you've seen her?

NATASHA: Nearly a year.

MIRROR: That's a long time. Do you even know where she is?

NATASHA: She sends postcards from time to time.

MIRROR: Postcards?

NATASHA: She's gone travelling. She's probably in Thailand by now.

MIRROR: Probably?

NATASHA: That's where they all go nowadays, isn't it?

MIRROR: You used to be so close.

NATASHA: She was a real daddy's girl.

MIRROR: Not for a long time now. (*Pause*) Does he miss her?

NATASHA: He complains about the money whenever I wonder where she is, but that's all.

MIRROR: What happened?

NATASHA: I told her Tony wanted me to change the deeds of the house to joint ownership and that I was thinking about it. She went mad. She said I was a weak-minded fool and couldn't see what was in front of me unless he pointed it out. She said she couldn't stand it anymore and wouldn't set foot in this house until her father had moved out. It was such a shock, hearing the language that came out of her mouth. I had no idea she felt like that, that she even knew. [*Beat*] My little girl. [*Beat*] She used to be such a sweet thing. I mean, talking like that, about her own father!

[*Silence*]

MIRROR: It's nothing new. I've seen it all before.

NATASHA: Of course you have.

MIRROR: Do you know how old I am?

NATASHA: You were my grandmother's wedding present? Let's see, she was married at twenty, buried at seventy. She died twenty… no twenty-three years ago. That makes you seventy-three years old.

MIRROR: I am as old as the world itself.

NATASHA: That was my second answer.

MIRROR: Shall I tell you a story?

NATASHA: That's not really a question, is it?

MIRROR: When the world was young I was a mighty cliff that loved the sea. I knew it in all its moods. Though its tides and tempests confused and terrified me, I adored it for those rosy dawns when it lay calm beside me, lapping my outcrops and murmuring between my coves. How easy it was to forget the sting of recent storms on those mornings and the golden peace of sunset seemed to make everything worthwhile. It was several hundred years before I perceived how diminished I was. Changed beyond recognition, I didn't know myself. [*Beat*] A mighty rock no longer, I had been reduced to mere sand; the plaything of the sea.

NATASHA: Now look at you.

MIRROR: Now, look at you.

NATASHA: No, please don't.

MIRROR: Did it hurt this time?

NATASHA: What? Oh…I…yes, it did… I wasn't prepared.

MIRROR: The last time wasn't the last time after all?

NATASHA: No. [*Pause*] But it hasn't happened for a long time, and he was sorry immediately afterwards.

MIRROR: Oh well, that's alright then, isn't it? I suppose that's why he's taking you out tonight?

NATASHA: Yes.

MIRROR: That's a new dress.

NATASHA: Yes.

MIRROR: You weren't always so easily won.

NATASHA: It was my fault really.

MIRROR: Oh aye?

NATASHA: Well, you know what he's like. He was tired, I should have left it.

MIRROR: What did you say?

NATASHA: I asked him what had kept him so late. It was none of my business.

MIRROR: You are his wife.

NATASHA: I'm a nag.

MIRROR: Natasha?

MIRROR: Yes?

MIRROR: Oh, it is you. For a moment I thought I was speaking to the husband.

NATASHA: No, it's still me.

MIRROR: Are you sure? It's getting harder to tell the difference. I've known you for a long time yet I recognise you less and less every day. Where's the girl who plaited her hair and wore mini-skirts in all weathers?

NATASHA: She's still here

MIRROR: No, her reflection is all that's left. An echo of what was, what could have been. A shadow creeps to the glass searching for its lost self, an Ahania weeping for her Urizen, and I give back what I can. Out of pity. It's a poor effort. I have only the past and future to work with, the present is too close to see, and a mirror has a bad memory. I see your form but there's no substance.

NATASHA: What do mirrors show but forms?

MIRROR: I suppose you would say that, it is understandable. In your brief, mortal world you see only physical forms. You congratulate yourselves on your mastery of your environment but in truth you see only a fraction of it. Your mortal eyes see only the mortal world but that isn't all. Standing in this room you believe yourself to be alone but you aren't. Around you the space is thronged with echoes, of the past, the future – your grandmother is among them, safe now. They are radiant but you are blind to them. I see more than I show and I show more than you see. But I have my limitations for I need light.

NATASHA: There's plenty of light in this room.

MIRROR: It is the light of the soul I need. Babies dazzle with it, the intensity dims a little as experience tempers innocence but there's none left in you. [*Pause*] Poor girl, I wanted better for you. I expected better of you.

NATASHA: Well that's your problem. Why should I care about your expectations? My whole life has been weighed down by expectations. I'm sick to death of them. Grandma expects, mummy expects, England expects?! They'd sit in this room and tell me my future. My objections and worries were laughed off or brushed aside. It frightened me. Their every utterance

41

promised exile. Even the boyfriends I was cheerfully assured of took on the sinister aspect of strangers, taking me away from everything I knew, everyone I loved. I think they thought there was something wrong with me when I cried at their scrying, but I was frightened. I didn't want to grow up and go away. I wanted to stay as I was, safe and in control of my own world. [*Beat*] I had such a terror of being sent away. It was a relief to find Tony. He seemed to understand. We were the same, him and me; lost souls looking for shelter. We needed each other and we clung to each other. Suddenly it didn't matter what Mummy and Grandma said; Tony was my whole world. I couldn't be sent away from myself. [*Beat*] We were so happy.

MIRROR: When did it go wrong?

NATASHA: I don't know.

MIRROR: Yes you do. You cannot lie to me.

NATASHA: The business got into trouble a few years ago. In fact he went bankrupt. That's how he found out about this house. [*Beat*] It was a very difficult time, he got so depressed. Every day he told me to leave him. "Why don't you just go?" He'd say, "Just fuck off, there's nothing more for you here." What could I do? I was his wife, I loved him, there was no question of leaving him. [*Beat*] I should never have told him that.

MIRROR: Why?

NATASHA: That was the first time he hit me. [*Beat*] That hardly matters; it was his words that hurt most. He told me I was manipulative, like all women, that I enjoyed seeing him down, knowing I owned the house we lived in while he wasn't allowed even a credit card. He accused me of lording it over him. He wouldn't believe I loved him when he'd lost everything.

MIRROR: Now you're lost.

NATASHA: All gone. Only this house remains. When I got married, grandma made me promise that I'd keep the house in my name, however difficult things became. I kept that promise and it has cost me everything.

MIRROR: Then why keep it?

NATASHA: Because when she came to me that day I saw something in her eyes… such impossible sadness.

MIRROR: That was always there.

NATASHA: I know, but when I was little I used to think she was sad because Granddad had died, but it never faded. As I grew older it seemed to take on a life of its own, as though the pain of a thousand years had found its expression through her. She was the face of every woman the world has ever known who has survived a catastrophe only to discover that everything and everyone she held dear was lost forever. And on my wedding day she turned her eyes on me.

MIRROR: She didn't like Tony

NATASHA: I despised her that day. Even though she had just given me everything I despised her for her silent grief. She frightened me. I didn't want to hear her warnings or see her promise of pain. It was my special day. I didn't understand, I just thought, "Even now you can't be happy for me. Isn't this what you wanted? I've got the man, I'm getting married. You can't even smile at me. The happiest day of my life and I'm still a disappointment." Tony smiled though. When I saw him standing at the altar smiling at me I knew I was safe. I knew he'd look after me.

MIRROR: And now?

NATASHA: Now I understand. She was terrified for my sake.

MIRROR: She saw what was to come. She knew that your husband and hers had been cut from the same cloth.

NATASHA: Granddad?

MIRROR: What do you remember?

NATASHA: Hardly anything. Whispered silences… dark, sterile corridors… an old man in a hospital bed… Mummy holding my hand too tight. After he died we came to live here and his name was never mentioned.

MIRROR: Your grandmother owned nothing during her husband's lifetime; she inherited her own house on his death. She could do nothing without his permission. She has given you the means to take control of your life.

NATASHA: I nearly agreed to the joint ownership. If Emma hadn't kicked up such a fuss. [*Beat*] he still won't let it go.

MIRROR: Don't go tonight.

NATASHA: What?

MIRROR: If you go out with that man tonight you will lose everything.

NATASHA: My husband?

MIRROR: You cling to that title as though your life depended on it. The vows he made don't define what he is.

NATASHA: It'll be fine. We're going out to dinner, he has promised he won't drink, that it's all behind us now. It'll be alright. Won't it?

MIRROR: Tell me, as you sit there painting out his last slip, how often has he kept these promises? How often has he broken them?

NATASHA: That's not fair.

MIRROR: What do you know about fair? You excuse the inexcusable while blaming those who loved you for daring to hope you would be a success. Is this really what you think or is it just what your husband has taught you to think?

NATASHA: I don't know. I feel so confused. I don't know who I am anymore. Sometimes, when I look in the mirror, I don't recognise the woman staring back at me. It's just a ghost in the glass.

MIRROR: Ah. [*Pause*] You used to be so sure of yourself.

NATASHA: You mean opinionated.

MIRROR: You had the courage of your convictions.

NATASHA: I made my bed.

[*Silence*]

MIRROR: Before you were married you wrote something on my glass. Do you remember what it was?

NATASHA: No.

MIRROR: You answer too quickly. Are you sure? [*Natasha looks away*] In lipstick you wrote, "I would die for Tony Marks". Blood-red it was.

NATASHA: I was in love.

MIRROR: And now?

NATASHA: I still love him.

MIRROR: He's killing you.

NATASHA: I know.

[*Silence*]

MIRROR: You know?

NATASHA: I stopped living a long time ago.

MIRROR: Then why stay?

NATASHA: Because I've seen the man he's capable of being. The man he can become, with my support. I just need to hang in there a little longer.

MIRROR: It's never going to happen. It's a foolish woman who expects a man to change. You must get clear of him.

NATASHA: But this is my home, where would I go?

MIRROR: This is your house, make him go. Change the locks if you have to.

NATASHA: I can't.

MIRROR: You can and you must.

NATASHA: It's more than my life's worth.

MIRROR: No, it's exactly what your life's worth. Remember your grandmother?

NATASHA: I...

MIRROR: I have seen your past-

NATASHA: Please.

MIRROR: I can show you your future.

NATASHA: No! I don't want to see it.

MIRROR: You've already written it. There's prophecy in mirror-writing.

NATASHA: Then what's the point?

MIRROR: You've written *a* future. You can choose whether it's *your* future.

NATASHA: How?

MIRROR: Pick up the phone and call a locksmith, call the police.

NATASHA: Oh I couldn't. [*Hesitates*]

MIRROR: You are following in your grandmother's footsteps. You have a daughter, do you want her to follow in yours?

[*Silence*]

MIRROR: Where's your phone?

NATASHA: [*Picking it up from the dressing table*] I have it here.

MIRROR: I'll leave it up to you then. It's your choice.

[*Sound of car pulling up outside. Car door opens and closes. Natasha gets up and looks out of the window. Lights down on mirror. As Natasha speaks, her expression reflects what she sees below.*]

NATASHA: Oh here he is! He looks happy. Oh yes [*looks at her watch*] we'd better go.

MIRROR: How long before he begins to hiss?

NATASHA: [*Ignoring Mirror, calling to Tony*] I won't be long darling! [*To the Mirror, behind her*] It's fine. It'll be fine.

MIRROR: And tomorrow? And the day after that? Will it always be fine?

[*She continues to look out through the window, the relief has gone from her face, she's nervous.*]

MIRROR: It's up to you.

[*Natasha looks upstage. Lights up on mirror. The mirrored surface has been replaced by an opaque surface (or the tin-foil surface has been turned around). Written across the glass, in blood-red lipstick, are the words "I would die for Tony Marks". There is a knock at the door. Natasha looks at the phone in her hand, then at the mirror, then at the door.*]

BLACKOUT

PERSPECTIVE

PERSPECTIVE

CHARACTERS OF THE PLAY

Bride: female; 20s – 30s
Bridesmaid: female; 20s – 30s
Couturier: female; 40+ French speaking (this can either
be genuinely French or clearly faked).

[*Two girls in dressing gowns in a dressing room. The Bride is standing before the mirror, agonising over her figure. Throughout the play she will move about the stage but will catch sight of herself in the mirror at intervals and the agonising will start all over again. The Bridesmaid is sitting stage front with her back to the Bride, flicking through a wedding magazine.*]

BRIDE: I don't think I shall eat anything more until the wedding.

BRIDESMAID: You'll die.

BRIDE: I want to look pale and fragile. I want to be [*Beat*] ethereally beautiful.

BRIDESMAID: The Corpse Bride. Michael's a lucky man.

BRIDE: That's horrible! I just want to be thin. What's wrong with that? [*Spans her waist with her hands*] My waist measurement should be less than my age.

BRIDESMAID: Not difficult.

BRIDE: Every bride wants to be thin on her wedding day.

BRIDESMAID: Not eating is a bit extreme. Your groom should carry you over the threshold because it's tradition, not because you're unconscious.

BRIDE: It's only a few days.

BRIDESMAID: You could be dead in a few days.

BRIDE: I've eaten a few carrots.

BRIDESMAID: So, you can *see* the pounds falling off?

BRIDE: It means I'll enjoy the wedding breakfast more.

BRIDESMAID: The bride looked beautiful as she glided

down the aisle towards her intended, but made a pig of herself at the reception. I've said it before and I'll say it again, Michael's a lucky man.

[*The Bride is about to reply but before she does so the Couturier enters.*]

COUTURIER: Ah, mademoiselle, I am so sorry to keep you waiting. The dresses are being prepared for you. One wedding and one bridesmaid, is that correct?

BRIDESMAID: Oui madame, vous avez raison.

COUTURIER: Ah, vous parlez francaise?

BRIDEMAID: Un petit peu, madame, oui.

COUTURIER: Ah! C'est tres bien! [*to Bridesmaid*] Your friend is a very talented woman.

[*exit*]

BRIDE: Show off.

BRIDESMAID: I've been brushing up on my French.

BRIDE: I should have been doing that, we're honeymooning in Antibes! Ooh, just think. In three days' time I'll be Mrs Richardson!

BRIDESMAID: Hoorah.

BRIDE: Oh it'll happen for you too. I'll make sure I throw the bouquet at you on Saturday.

BRIDESMAID: I'm not much of a catch-

BRIDE: [*Interrupting*] Oh don't say that. What you lack in physical attractiveness you make up for in personality.

BRIDESMAID: Catch*er*. I'm not much of a *catcher*. Bad hand-eye co-ordination.

BRIDE: Oh. [*Pause*] You have lovely hair.

BRIDESMAID: Thanks.

BRIDE: You bringing anyone?

BRIDESMAID: [*focusing once again on her magazine*] Nope.

BRIDE: Oh.

BRIDESMAID: Don't worry, he was never part of the plan. It won't upset your catering.

BRIDE: No, no, I wasn't thinking about that at all. But I thought you were quite keen on this one.

BRIDESMAID: Yes, I was. Yet we never even went on a proper date.

BRIDE: Though you certainly tried hard enough.

BRIDESMAID: Alright!

BRIDE: So, are you finally going to tell me what happened?

BRIDESMAID: I finally ran out of excuses for him.

BRIDE: What did he do?

BRIDESMAID: He said I was manipulative.

BRIDE: You? You're not even subtle!

BRIDESMAID: Apparently I was manipulating him with what I said and the way I dressed.

BRIDE: Poor man, I bet he can't order in a restaurant without feeling interrogated. Never mind, there are plenty more fish in the sea.

BRIDESMAID: I think someone's claiming my quota.

BRIDE: Well there's more to life than being in a relationship.

BRIDESMAID: Only people in a relationship say that.

BRIDE: But it's true. You have so much free time.

BRIDESMAID: Don't I know it!

BRIDE: But you can do what you like, go where you like. Where was it you went last year? Venice? Vancouver?

BRIDESMAID: Venezuala.

BRIDE: Yes! I knew it was somewhere I couldn't spell. You don't know how lucky you are. You have such freedom.

BRIDESMAID: Three words. Single Room Supplement.

BRIDE: I don't know what that is but what I'm saying is [*Beat*] I wanted Michael to propose to me in Prague but he refused to set foot in Eastern Europe. He thinks he'll be kidnapped.

BRIDESMAID: He does know the Cold War's over?

BRIDE: I think so. But he's seen that many films with James Mason in a trench coat he's developed a bit of a complex.

[*Bridesmaid picks up her handbag, takes out her phone and looks at it.*]

BRIDE: After what he said to you, you're still hoping he'll ring?

BRIDESMAID: Stupid isn't it? I know he won't.

BRIDE: I don't suppose it's even occurred to him to ring.

BRIDESMAID: I know, I just can't bear to think he's somewhere in the world thinking badly of me.

BRIDE: That's from Jane Austen isn't it?

BRIDESMAID: She's out of copyright.

BRIDE: I wouldn't worry about it. I'm sure he's not thinking badly of you.

BRIDESMAID: No?

BRIDE: He's probably forgotten all about you.

BRIDESMAID: Bastard.

BRIDE: What about that neighbour of yours? You thought he liked you.

BRIDESMAID: I'm not sure how I feel about him.

BRIDE: Oh well, if you're going to be fussy…

[*Silence. Bridesmaid looks at Bride*]

BRIDESMAID: You love Michael, don't you?

BRIDE: Yes, of course I do. That's why I'm marrying him.

BRIDESMAID: And you fancy him too?

BRIDE: Yes.

BRIDESMAID: Then why do you think I should settle for

anything less?

[*Silence*]

BRIDESMAID: Call me old fashioned but I want a man I love and desire. To settle for anything less is just whoring and I would no sooner settle for a man for the sake of having one than I would saddle myself with a lifetime of debt for a grotty flat in a bad part of town just to be able to call it mine.

BRIDE: Love comes at a price you know.

BRIDESMAID: Oh yes, what price?

BRIDE: Football.

BRIDESMAID: Football?

BRIDE: Every Saturday during the season, the house is invaded and the living room taken over by Michael and his mates. They trample the sofa and scream at the telly for an hour and a half and then disappear to the pub to drown their sorrows. That's when I think of you sitting all by yourself in your rented room and think how lucky you are.

BRIDESMAID: Lucky?

BRIDE: You have nothing and nobody. You pass through life quite unnoticed. If I miss my train on the way home, Michael phones me to find out where I am. It's like I'm not my own person any more. I'm somebody's other half. Sometimes I have these nightmares that I'm dissolving, melting, slowly ceasing to be. I almost dread to look at family photos in case I'm fading out of them.

BRIDESMAID: Wedding nerves. That's all it is.

BRIDE: Do you think so?

BRIDESMAID: That and you watch too many films. You're not Marty McFly!

BRIDE: Possibly. But much as you might hate always being on your own, it's not much fun never being on your own. And you do have fun.

BRIDESMAID: Oh yes, I haven't lost the will to live just yet.

BRIDE: What are you doing for Christmas?

BRIDESMAID: I'm meeting up with some friends in Rome. You?

BRIDE: Mother-in-law.

BRIDESMAID: Oh God.

BRIDE: It's not so unreasonable, I suppose. She's on her own now…

BRIDESMAID: But?

BRIDE: But every time we go down there Michael regresses to the role of Number 1 Son. She makes such a fuss of him that I feel like some sort of interloper. I can't say anything to him. You can't criticise a man's mother, only he can do that. The worst thing is that after a weekend at her house, he expects the same treatment from me when we get home.

BRIDESMAID: Better snap him out of that quick.

BRIDE: Oh I do, believe me. I remind him of a few things that his mother doesn't do for him. [*Beat*] That usually does the trick, though sometimes it puts him off for days. [*Beat*] I really wanted to have our first Christmas at home, just the two of us.

BRIDESMAID: I suppose you don't just marry the man.

BRIDE: No.

BRIDESMAID: Let's just hope the mother-in-law doesn't snore!

BRIDE: I shouldn't moan. She's not that bad.

BRIDESMAID: Of course she isn't.

BRIDE: And she won't live forever.

BRIDESMAID: [*Beat*] No.

BRIDE: Don't look at me like that! I wasn't proposing to do her in; the Bride, in the kitchen, with the Quiche Lorraine.

BRIDESMAID: More my role, isn't it? Embittered old spinster, with the knitting needles?

BRIDE: You'll meet someone.

BRIDESMAID: [*Beat*] I tried internet dating once.

BRIDE: And?

BRIDESMAID: Someone contacted me, a guy.

BRIDE: You never told me this! Was he nice?

BRIDESMAID: I can't remember. Anyway, he said he wasn't too sure about internet dating and I said…

BRIDE: What did you say?

BRIDESMAID: I said "Yes I know, it's a bit like selling yourself on eBay, isn't it?"

BRIDE: You didn't hear from him again, did you?

BRIDESMAID: No.

BRIDE: No one at work?

BRIDESMAID: No. The single guys are either 25 or 55.

BRIDE: Age isn't important.

BRIDESMAID: It is to them!

BRIDE: You should go to more dinner parties.

BRIDESMAID: Dinner parties? A bit old fashioned aren't they? They belong to a time when people could still afford to buy houses.

BRIDE: You're being silly.

BRIDESMAID: [*Takes a deep breath, preparing for a speech*] A one-bedroom flat in greater London costs £900 to rent, more if you want one big enough to take furniture. Add council tax and bills, there's hardly any money left for food. To throw a dinner party you need space! That's why Downton Abbey is so popular. It's got nothing to do with the clothes and everything to do with the sight of a large group of people eating at the same table with no one wedged against the wall or perched on a kitchen chair. [*As she speaks, Bridesmaid moves around the stage.*] The talk is accompanied only by the tinkling of cut glass crystal and so the conversation can flow sweetly because, as we all know, nothing kills the chat quite like the sound of someone pissing on the other side of the wall. Especially if the poor unfortunate fighting with the flush wasn't the first to get up! Alas, that life is for the rich. For me, the carpet picnic, mindful of course of any stains that might risk the deposit. [*Beat*] What I resent most is that I work hard in a well-paid job that simply doesn't buy anything. Living alone in London is unsustainable. Perhaps I am to blame, though. For which of us didn't read *Pride & Prejudice* and wish that life was a bit more like a Jane Austen novel? Well, know it is. Finding a man has become almost an economic necessity.

[*Silence*]

BRIDE: If Michael and I *ever* have a dinner party, we'll invite you.

BRIDESMAID: You won't. Couples don't mix with singles.

BRIDE: Rubbish.

BRIDESMAID: It's true. Take me and you, for example. We're pretty close, aren't we?

BRIDE: I wouldn't have asked anyone else to be my bridesmaid.

BRIDESMAID: Exactly. And no one but me would have agreed to wear that dress. OK, we're close. We've known each other a long time. I've held your hair while you've been sick and you've held mine.

BRIDE: We've shared the details of our…romantic escapades.

BRIDESMAID: You've gone into so much detail I've wanted to light up afterwards.

BRIDE: Alright, alright…

BRIDESMAID: And now, here we are the culmination of

all your hopes and dreams, feminism notwithstanding, The Wedding.

BRIDE: Ah!

[*Bride swirls around happily, hugging herself in her excitement, then catches sight of herself in the mirror*

and stills, scrutinising herself.]

BRIDESMAID: And I'm pleased for you, I really am, but it is the end of us.

BRIDE: No!

BRIDESMAID: [*Pause*] Do you know how I knew Michael was special?

BRIDE: Because I told you about him [*lowers her dressing gown before the mirror to examine her upper arms*].

BRIDESMAID: Because you *didn't* tell me about him. Within weeks of meeting him you suffered an unprecedented attack of decorum. I didn't get one juicy detail out of you as far as he was concerned. It was quite a shock to the system. I almost went into withdrawal.

BRIDE: Don't exaggerate.

BRIDESMAID: Suddenly I was the enemy. It wasn't you and me against all comers any more, it was all about you and Michael and you were going to protect that at all costs. I wasn't a confidante any more, I was a threat.

BRIDE: That isn't true. [*Leans forward to examine her cleavage*].

BRIDESMAID: But it is and it's not just you. Single girls on a night out can hardly go to the toilet without a support group but once she's got a man every single friend is competition. They all want what she's got. It's every girl for herself; friendship is only make-up deep.

BRIDE: I never saw you as competition.

BRIDESMAID: Couples herd together for safety. The women who were once our comrades in arms now pull up the ladder after them and sit in their matrimonial towers shouting down to the rest of us that there are lots of lovely guys out there without being able to introduce a single man who is actually single. They're not offering comfort, they're really saying "Keep away!" And that's the reason they keep us at arm's length; we become a threat to their "happy state". Single men disappear when they hit thirty. Women become aloof the moment they're coupled.

BRIDE: It hasn't been like that with us.

BRIDESMAID: Oh no?

BRIDE: Well, obviously things have changed and it's not going to be exactly the same but…

BRIDESMAID: I give us six months.

BRIDE: Can I pay a fine instead?

BRIDESMAID: We won't fall out or anything like that; we'll still send Christmas cards. It's just that I'll, gradually, become irrelevant; like that spandex mini skirt you bought the day we got our A' Level results.

BRIDE: You're the only one who knows about that, you mustn't leave me. You're my best friend. Look, you're just a bit down over what's-his-name. You'll meet someone new and we'll go on as before.

BRIDESMAID: You know, I'm not sure I'm the sort of girl men fall in love with. I mean, if you want your dinner cooked or the tea made, or an outing organised, I'm top of the list. But, otherwise, no one gives me a second thought.

[*Pause*]

BRIDE: You did a cracking job on that Hen Night. It was such a great night.

BRIDESMAID: It was, wasn't it? I was rather pleased with that. One of my best, I'd say. Butler in the Buff not too much?

BRIDE: Oh no.

BRIDESMAID: Good. I've booked him again for your wedding night. [*Off Bride's look*] I'm kidding.

BRIDE: Are you? Right. [*Beat*] He was good [*Beat*] It was such fun! Though I'm relieved you didn't make us all wear "L" plates.

BRIDESMAID: A Hen Night is no place for irony.

[*Bride looks at her as though unsure how to react.*]

BRIDE: Well, I really enjoyed it. The club was great.

BRIDESMAID: It's a shame no one wanted to dance.

BRIDE: None of us were quite drunk enough.

BRIDESMAID: It's such a shame.

BRIDE: The drinks were really expensive!

BRIDESMAID: No, I mean this idea that we have to be drunk before we do anything. It wasn't always like that was it? I remember our school discos. It was a can of Tizer and a packet of Golden Wonder and we never got off the dance floor.

BRIDE: We were eight.

BRIDESMAID: I know, but now we're all so obsessed with appearances that no one will dance or sing without having their excuse lined up.

BRIDE: Appearances are everything

BRIDESMAID: Well they shouldn't be; that belief has more reach than Facebook. It censures everything. No one dares give in to the joy of the moment unless they can dismiss it all the next day by saying "I was drunk". It's so sad. Nothing's allowed to be fun anymore.

BRIDE: I had fun. I always was a rebel.

BRIDESMAID: We have sex where we may once just have shaken hands and that's all fine but the thought of taking to the dance floor while sober has somehow become the mark of the eccentric.

BRIDE: When Marie dances you can see why she doesn't want to remember the experience. Having seen her, I'm not sure I want to remember it.

BRIDESMAID: You'll be deleting those photos then?

BRIDE: Blatantly not! It's her birthday next month.

BRIDESMAID: She'll love that.

BRIDE: What are friends for?

BRIDESMAID: So, is everything else done?

BRIDE: [*Sitting down beside Bridesmaid*] Yes, more or less. I suppose there will be some last minute catastrophe but the seating plan's done, thank God! There's something very odd about planning a wedding breakfast around so many divorced couples. Their wants and needs dominate everything. I suppose if I allowed myself to dwell on it too much I'd think better of the whole thing.

BRIDESMAID: Too late now.

BRIDE: I know. We'd have to send the presents back. We've got some rather nice things.

BRIDESMAID: Not from me you haven't. I'm making you something.

BRIDE: I'm sure it will be lovely. You're so accomplished.

BRIDESMAID: I also play the piano and speak French. I'm just waiting for someone dashing to swing down from his horse and claim me…

BRIDE: You read too many books.

BRIDESMAID: …though knowing my luck, the minute his foot touched the ground he'd age a thousand years and crumble to dust at my feet.

BRIDE: There just isn't the quality out there.

BRIDESMAID: No.

BRIDE: But you'd get to keep the horse.

BRIDESMAID: It wouldn't fit in the flat. [*Beat*] Better than a cat I suppose.

BRIDE: More expensive.

BRIDESMAID: But less likely to end up eating me. [*Beat*]

Are you keeping your name?

BRIDE: I wanted to but double-barrelling sounds a bit indecisive, like I'm hedging my bets.

BRIDESMAID: Then again…

BRIDE: What's in a name?

BRIDESMAID: Nothing I hope. His name's Pratt

BRIDE: And mine's Large

BRIDESMAID: Double-barrelling probably not the way to go.

BRIDE: No.

BRIDESMAID: Still, given the way things are these days, it's probably more acceptable to be a Pratt than a Large.

BRIDE: His mother would like that. She doesn't hold with women keeping their names.

BRIDESMAID: What about your mum?

BRIDE: She doesn't want to wear a hat.

BRIDESMAID: Oh dear.

BRIDE: His mother looks great in hats. She tells me every time she sees me. She thinks it gives her some sort of precedence over my mum.

BRIDESMAID: What about a fascinator?

BRIDE: Princess Beatrice killed the form. It's not fair; my mum is Mother of the Bride. This means almost more to her than it does to me. His mother should back off.

She's already got Christmas.

BRIDESMAID: What does Michael say?

BRIDE: Oh he's staying out of it. He doesn't want to know.

[*Pause, the Couturier bustles in with the wedding dress.*]

COUTURIER: Pardon, mes petites… Maintenant, [*Looks from one to the other*] who is the lucky girl?

[*Bride & Bridesmaid look at each other.*]

BLACKOUT

ABOUT THE AUTHOR

Julia Lee Dean holds a degree in English & Italian Literature from the University of Warwick and a Masters in History of Medicine & Science from Birkbeck College, University of London and was a member of the Yourg Writers' Programme at the Royal Court Theatre before training as an actress at Rose Bruford College.